Favorite Recipes FROM HAWAII

Cooking with Hawaiian flavor is enjoyable because island cuisine offers a variety of ethnic experiences. For those who have enjoyed these delicious delights and wish to share them with family and friends, here is an excellent collection of island favorites.

Each recipe is authentic, simple to do, and sure to win you fame. Successful Hawaiian Style entertaining depends upon plenty of Aloha . . . meaning good fun with good friends.

Aloha.

Table of Contents

Diamond Head, OAHU

PUPUS AND TROPICAL DRINKS

Hawaiian Sunset, OAHU

Paniola Meatballs with Barbecue Sauce

½ pound ground beef
½ pound ground pork
½ pound ground veal or turkey meat
½ cup chopped onions
2 eggs
1 cup fresh bread crumbs
1 tablespoon chopped mint
2 cloves garlic, finely chopped
½ cup chopped parsley
Salt and pepper to taste
Barbecue Sauce (recipe follows)

Combine all ingredients except barbecue sauce; mix well. Shape into meatballs, about 1½ inches in diameter. Bake meatballs for 20 minutes at 350°F or microwave for 10 minutes at high power. Meatballs may be made ahead and frozen. Reheat before serving. Serve Barbecue Sauce as a dip.

Barbecue Sauce

½ cup olive oil
2 cloves garlic, minced
½ cup red wine
¼ cup tomato paste
¼ cup fresh lemon juice
¼ cup chopped fresh basil
1 hot red chili pepper
Salt and pepper to taste

Combine all ingredients in a heavy saucepan; simmer for 10 minutes over low heat. Serve warm as a dipping sauce for Paniola Meatballs.

Curried Chutney Dip

¼ cup mango chutney (see recipe pg. 56)
1 cup mayonnaise
1 to 2 teaspoons curry powder

Coarsely chop mango chutney. Combine mango chutney, mayonnaise and curry powder; blend well. Chill. Serve as a dip with assorted fresh vegetables. Makes 1¼ cups.

Teriyaki Meat Sticks

2 pound sirloin steak
½ cup soy sauce
3 tablespoons sugar
1 tablespoon dry sherry
½ teaspoon minced fresh ginger or
⅛ teaspoon powdered ginger
1 clove garlic, minced

Slice steak diagonally into 2 x 1 x ¼-inch strips. Combine all the remaining ingredients; marinate meat slices for 30 minutes. Thread slices on skewers. Barbecue or broil until done. Makes 48.

Grilled Jumbo Shrimp in Spicy Black Bean Sauce

5 pounds large shrimp (5 to 8 count)
½ cup fresh lemon juice
1 jar Chinese hot black bean paste

Clean shrimp and remove shells, leaving tails intact. Remove the vein without cutting into the shrimp by bending the shrimp and gently pull out the vein with a food pick, carefully moving it from side to side. Combine lemon juice and black bean paste. Pour the sauce over the shrimp; mix well. Start the coals and when the white ash stage has been reached, place the shrimp on the grill about 3 inches from the coals. Grill about 3 minutes on each side. Check one of the shrimp at 5 minutes. If it seems to be cooked and still very moist remove from the coals and serve at once with lots of paper napkins and cold beer. Makes 6 to 8 servings.

Island Shrimp Dip

2½ pounds small Pacific shrimp, cleaned and cooked
3 pkg. (8 oz. each) cream cheese, room temperature
½ cup sour cream
1½ cups mayonnaise
2 green onions, finely chopped
½ cup catsup
1 tablespoon seeded and chopped Hawaiian chili peppers
1 tablespoon Worcestershire sauce
1 teaspoon salt
½ teaspoon white pepper

Combine all ingredients; mix well. Chill. Serve with crisp crackers or with assorted fresh vegetables.

Chinatown Duck Pate in Terrine

2 ducks (4 to 5 pounds each)
½ cup brandy or Madeira
½ pound ground lean veal
1 pound ground lean pork
2 cloves garlic, minced
2 tablespoons finely chopped orange zest
1 teaspoon salt
½ teaspoon freshly ground pepper
1 bay leaf
1 pound bacon, 6 ounces caul fat or cheese cloth to line terrine
12 ounces pork fat or hard back fat, cut into 3 x ¼-inch strips

Cut ducks into quarters; remove skin and bones. Freeze the bones. Cut duck meat into thin strips. Pour brandy over the meat; mix well and set aside for 1 hour. In a bowl combine veal, pork, garlic, orange zest, salt and pepper; mix well. Line a 2-quart terrine or loaf pan with bacon, caul fat or cheese cloth. Line the bottom of the terrine with one third of the pork fat strips. Add half the ground meat mixture and half of the duck. Add one third of the pork fat in the middle, a layer of duck, then the ground meat mixture. End with last one third of the pork fat on the top. Place the bay leaf in the center. Bring the bacon, caul fat or cheese cloth over the top of the mixture. Cover the terrine or loaf pan with foil or a tight fitting cover. Place terrine in a deep dish half full of hot water in an oven preheated to 350°F for 1½ hours. Replace water in pan as needed, use boiling water. When baked, remove from the water bath and take off cover. Place the terrine on a baking sheet to catch excess juices; cover with foil and weigh the terrine down with weights or heavy cans. Refrigerate overnight or several days. When ready to serve remove from the terrine and slice thinly. Serve with melba toast, mustards and sour pickles. Makes 8 servings.

Crispy Wun Tun

¼ pound raw shrimp
½ pound ground pork
⅓ cup minced bamboo shoots (optional)
6 water chestnuts, minced
2 tablespoons thinly sliced green onions
2 tablespoons soy sauce
¼ teaspoon minced fresh ginger or
⅛ teaspoon powdered ginger
1 egg, lightly beaten
1 pkg. (10 oz.) wun tun wrappers
Oil for deep frying
Oriental Dipping Sauce (recipe follows)

Peel and devein shrimp; finely chop. Combine shrimp, ground pork, bamboo shoots, water chestnuts, green onions, soy sauce, ginger and egg; mix lightly to blend. Place 1 teaspoon of the shrimp mixture in center of each wun tun wrapper; dampen edges with water and fold diagonally, sealing well. With straight edge at top, dampen right point and fold left point under it, pinching to seal. Roll center point towards the back to form a packet. Heat oil for deep frying to 375°F. Fry wun tun 3 to 4 minutes or until golden brown. Serve with Oriental Dipping Sauce. Makes 48.

Oriental Dipping Sauce

2 teaspoons dry mustard
1 teaspoon warm water
¾ cup soy sauce

In a small bowl stir together mustard and warm water to make a smooth paste. Invert bowl on plate for 15 minutes to increase strength of mustard. Stir soy sauce into mustard paste just before serving. Makes ¾ cup.

Vegetable Tempura

Combination of the following vegetables:
- Green beans or string beans, parboil for 5 minutes and cut into 2-inch lengths
- Sweet potatoes, peeled and thinly sliced
- Carrots and celery, cut in thin diagonal slices
- Eggplant, cut into ¼-inch slices
- Fresh mushrooms, sliced
- Watercress and spinach, cut into small bunches
- Lotus root, peeled and thinly sliced

Oil for deep frying
½ cup flour
½ cup cornstarch
1 egg, beaten
⅔ cup ice water
Sweet-Sour Dipping Sauce (recipe follows)

Rinse vegetables and pat dry on paper towels. Heat oil for deep frying to 375°F. Combine flour and cornstarch. Blend together egg and water; stir into flour mixture, mixing only until blended. Dip vegetables into batter and fry 2 minutes or until lightly browned. Drain on absorbent paper. Serve with Sweet-Sour Dipping Sauce.

Sweet-Sour Dipping Sauce

¾ cup sugar
2 tablespoons soy sauce
¼ cup white vinegar
¼ cup catsup
2 tablespoons cornstarch
½ cup ice water

Combine sugar, soy sauce, white vinegar and catsup in a heavy saucepan; bring to boil. Mix the cornstarch and water to make a smooth paste and stir into sauce. Cook until thickened, stirring constantly.

Seviche Maui-Style

1½ pounds sea scallops
1 pound firm white fish, cut into 1-inch squares
Lemon, lime or a combination of lemon and lime juice, to cover the fish
1 cup coarsely chopped bell peppers
1 cup small wedges of Maui onions
2 tomatoes, peeled, seeded and cut into wedges
1 to 2 hot red chili peppers, seeded and finely chopped
1 tablespoon Worcestershire sauce

Combine all ingredients and marinate overnight. When ready to serve drain off the liquid from the fish and sprinkle 1 cup chopped parsley over the top. Serve with fresh hot French bread.

Stuffed Oysters on the Half Shell

½ cup unsalted sweet cream butter
1 cup dried bread crumbs
3 cloves garlic, minced
3 cups chopped parsley
5 pounds rock salt
36 fresh oysters in the shell, allow 6 per person

Combine butter, bread crumbs, garlic and parsley; blend well. Spread rock salt on baking sheets or in ovenproof dishes for serving. Place in a very hot oven until you are ready to run the oysters under the broiler. Scrub oysters under running water. Open oysters and top with a well rounded tablespoon of the crumb mixture. Place on the hot salt and then under the broiler until the stuffing is hot. Serve immediately.

Pacific Clams in Garlic

Fresh clams, allow 6 to 8 clams per person as a luncheon dish
1 cup fresh lemon juice
¼ cup chopped garlic
Salt and freshly ground black pepper

Small little neck clams are nice to grill over hot coals. Place the clams on the grill rack, close to the coals, and grill until the clams open. If you wish to remove the top shell of the clam when open, use heavy gloves or pot holders while you pry the tops off. Be careful not to spill the juices from the bottom clam shell. Combine lemon juice and garlic. Place about ½ teaspoon of the lemon mixture on the clams. Sprinkle with salt and pepper.

Note: This mixture works well on mussels or oysters. You may wish to have a combination of clams, mussels and oysters with several dipping sauces and serve as party pupus. On a large platter have hot chopped chili peppers, lime and lemon wedges, barbecue sauce, soy sauce and flavored vinegars. Everyone can make his own sauces.

Mai Tai

½ ounce fresh lime juice
½ ounce orange curacao
½ ounce Hawaiian Cane Syrup (recipe follows)
¼ ounce orgeat syrup
1½ ounce light rum
½ ounce dark rum
Cracked ice
1 ounce Lemon Hart rum (86)

In a double old fashioned glass combine lime juice, orange curacao, Hawaiian Cane Syrup, orgeat syrup, light rum and dark rum; stir well. Add cracked ice to fill glass. Gently pour Lemon Hart rum on top to float on surface. Makes 1 drink.

Idea: Garnish with fresh pineapple wedge, vanda orchid and sprig of fresh mint, if desired.

Banana Daiquiri

1 banana, cut into chunks
3 ounces light rum
1 tablespoon fresh lemon juice
1 ounce Hawaiian Cane Syrup (recipe follows)
2 cups cracked ice

Process banana in a blender or electric drink mixer until smooth. Add rum, lemon juice, Hawaiian Cane Syrup and cracked ice; blend to a slushy consistency. Pour into two daiquiri glasses. Makes 2 drinks.

Hawaiian Cane Syrup
(Simple Syrup)

Combine equal amounts of sugar and water and bring to a boil. Boil 5 minutes, stirring occasionally. Chill.

Chi Chi

1 wedge fresh pineapple
3 ounces pineapple juice
1 ounce coconut syrup
½ ounce fresh lemon juice
3 ounces vodka
1 cup cracked ice

Process fresh pineapple in a blender or electric drink mixer until smooth. Add pineapple juice, coconut syrup, lemon juice, vodka and cracked ice; blend well. Pour into two highball glasses. Makes 2 drinks.

Idea: Garnish with fresh pineapple wedge, vanda orchid and a sprig of fresh mint, if desired.

Tropical Fruit Punch

1 cup sugar
2 cups boiling water
2 cups strong tea, chilled
2 cups pineapple juice
½ cup fresh lemon juice
12 ounces rum
28 ounces ginger ale, chilled

Dissolve sugar in boiling water; cool. Add all the remaining ingredients. Serve over a decorative ice mold, if desired. Makes 3 quarts.

SOUPS AND SALADS

Kapalua, MAUI

Tropical Pineapple Boat

Cut pineapple in half lengthwise through crown, leaving crown intact. Remove fruit from pineapple halves, leaving ½-inch of fruit inside the shell. Cut fruit into cubes. Toss pineapple cubes lightly with a selection of tropical fruits (i.e., banana, papaya, kiwi, mango, watermelon, etc.). Spoon into pineapple boats to serve.

Portuguese Bean Soup

3 ham hocks
2 quarts beef broth or water
2 large onions, sliced
1 mild Portuguese sausage, sliced
4 cloves garlic, minced
4 large potatoes, diced
2 carrots, sliced
6 fresh ripe tomatoes, chopped
¼ cup basil leaves
2 bay leaves
1 can (13 oz.) tomato sauce
2 bunches watercress, cut into 1-inch pieces
4 cups canned pinto or kidney beans
Salt and pepper to taste

Cover ham hocks with beef broth and simmer until tender. Remove ham hocks from the broth and allow to cool. When cool, remove the meat from the bones and cut into bite size pieces. Add onions, sausage, garlic, potatoes, carrots, tomatoes, basil and bay leaves to the broth. Simmer for 30 minutes. Add tomato sauce, watercress, pinto beans and the meat from the ham hocks. Cook another 20 minutes. Serve or refrigerate overnight or for several days. Reheat to serve.

Chilled Kona Cucumber Soup

2 large potatoes, peeled and diced
1 cup chicken stock
1 cup white wine
2 cucumbers, chopped
4 celery stalks, chopped
¼ cup chopped onion
1 teaspoon salt
Freshly ground black pepper
1 cup heavy cream
Mint for garnish

Cook the potatoes in the stock and white wine until soft, then add all of the remaining ingredients, except the heavy cream, and simmer for 5 minutes. Cool. Process the soup in a food processor or blender until smooth. Chill well. When ready to serve, add the cream. Serve the soup in chilled glass bowls for a very cool look. Garnish with a sprig of fresh mint if desired.

Egg Drop Soup

2 quarts rich chicken stock
6 eggs, beaten
½ teaspoon white pepper
1 teaspoon sesame oil
¼ cup chopped Chinese parsley

Bring chicken stock to a full boil in a stockpot. Beat together the eggs, white pepper and sesame oil. Turn off heat under the stock and slowly add the egg mixture in a steady stream. Let the eggs go to the bottom of the broth, then float back up to the top. The eggs will be in the shape of flowers and be very light and delicate in texture. Stir in the Chinese parsley and serve at once.

Honolulu Watercress Soup

1 package (10 oz.) frozen small peas (use fresh if in season)
5 cups rich beef stock
1 small onion, coarsely chopped
1 stalk celery, coarsely chopped
¼ cup butter
2 tablespoons flour
½ cup heavy cream
2 tablespoons chopped mint
2 cups chopped watercress
Salt and pepper to taste

Simmer peas and beef stock together for 5 minutes, then add onion and celery. Simmer another 5 minutes. Cool. Process soup in a food processor or blender until smooth. In a heavy saucepan melt butter; stir in flour and cook until mixture is light and bubbly. Pour the smooth pea mixture into the pan and cook until thickened. Add the heavy cream, mint and watercress. Season with salt and pepper. Serve hot and garnish with a sprig of fresh mint or watercress.

Pacific Bouillabaisse Salad

½ pound shrimp, peeled, deveined and cooked
½ pound lobster meat, cooked and diced
½ pound mahimahi, cooked and cubed
½ pound crab meat, cooked and flaked
2 dozen clams or mussels, steamed
1 cup fresh lemon juice
Salt and pepper to taste
1 head curly lettuce
1 head Romaine lettuce
12 to 16 cherry tomatoes, cut into roses
8 large ripe olives
1 bunch watercress
1 recipe Garlic Mayonnaise Dressing (recipe follows)

Combine shrimp, lobster, mahimahi, crab meat and clams with lemon juice, salt and pepper; toss gently. Chill. When ready to serve the salad, arrange the curly and Romaine lettuce leaves on chilled plates; top with seafood mixture and garnish with the tomatoes, olives and watercress. Pass the Garlic Mayonnaise Dressing. Serve with chilled wine and hot French bread.

Garlic Mayonnaise Dressing

2 eggs
2 teaspoons Dijon style mustard
4 cloves garlic
1 tablespoon chopped hot red chili peppers
Salt to taste
¼ cup fresh lemon juice
2 cups olive oil

In a blender or food processor place the eggs, mustard, garlic, hot chili peppers, salt and lemon juice. Blend a few minutes, then slowly add the olive oil. When the mixture has thickened, remove and refrigerate. It will thicken more as it chills.

Curried Seafood Salad

1 pound shrimp (about 12 to 15 count)
2 cups imitation crab or cooked and cubed lobster meat
2 cups cooked firm white fish, cut into bite size pieces
½ cup sliced celery
¼ cup sliced shallots
Curried Dressing (recipe follows)
Curly lettuce leaves
Several sprigs of watercress

Clean shrimp; remove shell and devein. Cook in boiling water for 2 minutes; drain. Carefully toss the seafood with celery and shallots. Chill. When ready to serve the salad, toss the seafood gently with the Curried Dressing. Serve on crisp curly lettuce leaves and garnish with sprigs of watercress.

Curried Dressing

1 cup mayonnaise
2 tablespoons coarsely chopped mango chutney
1 tablespoon curry powder
¼ cup heavy cream
2 tablespoons lemon juice

Combine all the ingredients; mix well. Chill.

Idea: Serve the following condiments with the salad — toasted coconut, toasted macadamia nuts and chopped green onions, if desired.

Big Island Salad with Fresh Herb Dressing

Gather your favorite salad greens . . . lettuce, spinach, horseradish leaves, onion and chive tops, radishes, avocadoes, mushrooms, cucumbers and tomatoes.

Break the greens into bite size pieces. Cut the other vegetables into wedges or slices. Chill until ready to serve. When ready to serve the salad sprinkle the Herb Salad Dressing over the vegetables and toss gently.

Herb Salad Dressing

2 cloves garlic
1 teaspoon salt
¼ cup fresh basil leaves
1 sprig marjoram
¼ cup vinegar
¾ cup olive oil

Place all ingredients, except olive oil, in a food processor or blender. Blend a few minutes, then slowly add the olive oil. Process until smooth. Refrigerate.

Kamuela Fennel and Mushroom Salad

3 heads Belgian endive, divided into leaves
2 large fennel bulbs, thinly sliced
12 large mushrooms, sliced
½ cup fresh lemon juice
Sea salt
Freshly ground black pepper

Place the endive leaves on chilled salad plates in a fan shape. In a bowl lightly toss fennel, mushrooms, lemon juice, sea salt and black pepper. Arrange the fennel and mushrooms on the endive leaves and serve at once.

Hawaiian Frozen Fruit Salad

1 package (8 oz.) cream cheese, room temperature
¼ cup sour cream
2 cups diced ripe mango
2 cups crushed pineapple, well drained
1 can lichee nuts
2 cups miniature marshmallows
1 cup chopped macadamia nuts
1 pint heavy cream
4 kiwi fruit, peeled and sliced

Oil a decorative mold. In a large bowl combine cream cheese and sour cream; mix together until light and fluffy. Fold in mango, pineapple, lichee nuts, marshmallows and macadamia nuts. Whip heavy cream until it holds stiff peaks, then fold into the cream cheese mixture. Pour half the mixture into the mold, then layer the sliced kiwi in the center; add the remaining cream cheese mixture. Cover the mold with foil and freeze until solid. This may be made several weeks in advance. One hour before serving the salad, unmold it by placing in warm water for a few minutes. Run a knife around the edge of the mold to let a little air in so the salad will drop out. Serve on a bed of mint leaves with clusters of green seedless grapes that have been dipped in egg white and sugar, if desired.

Idea: This salad can be made with any fresh fruits in season.

MAIN DISHES

Hawaii's Exotic Sky

Pacific Prawns with Watercress

4 pounds prawns
½ cup olive oil or clarified butter
1 cup coarsely chopped watercress
4 cloves garlic, minced
1 small Hawaiian red chili pepper, seeded and chopped
1 teaspoon salt
1 cup dry white wine

Clean prawns and remove shells, leaving tails intact. Remove the vein without cutting into the prawns by bending the prawns and gently pulling out the vein with a food pick, carefully moving it from side to side. In a heavy skillet heat the olive oil; add the prawns, watercress, garlic, Hawaiian pepper and salt. Cook the prawns until the flesh turns a lovely coral pink; add the wine and cook for another 5 minutes. The prawns are very nice served over cooked thin pasta and accompanied with fresh hot French bread.

Grilled Mahimahi on Skewers

4 pounds fresh or frozen mahimahi
4 green bell peppers
2 large Maui onions
24 10-inch bamboo skewers
1 jar (7 oz.) lilikoi jelly
½ cup soy sauce
1 teaspoon hot Chinese mustard
Salt and pepper to taste

Cut mahimahi into 1½-inch cubes. Cut bell peppers into 1-inch squares and blanch in boiling water for 1 minute. Cut Maui onions into wedges and separate into individual pieces. Thread the mahimahi, bell peppers and onions on to the skewers. In a heavy saucepan combine lilikoi jelly, soy sauce and hot Chinese mustard; heat to melt the jelly. Brush lilikoi sauce on the mahimahi and let set for 20 minutes. Have the coals in the grill at the white ash stage when you place the skewers on the grill. Grill on each side for about 7 minutes. Brush the fish several times with the lilikoi sauce. Serve with a fresh green salad and rice pilaf.

Grilled Shrimp and Scallops on Skewers with Green Sauce

Large shrimp (5 to 8 count), allow 6 per person
Bay scallops, allow 4 per person
Bamboo skewers
½ cup fresh lemon juice
Freshly ground black pepper
Salt
Green Sauce (recipe follows)

Clean shrimp and remove shells, leaving tails intact. Remove the vein from the shrimp without cutting into the shrimp by bending the shrimp and gently pulling out the vein with a food pick, carefully moving it from side to side. Rinse the scallops and pat dry. Thread shrimp and scallops onto skewers, starting and ending with a shrimp. Start the coals and when the white ash stage has been reached, place the skewers on the rack and grill for 3 to 4 minutes on each side. Brush well with lemon juice and grind pepper over the skewers as you turn them. Sprinkle with salt at the end of the cooking time. Serve with Green Sauce.

Green Sauce

1 egg
2 teaspoons Dijon style mustard
½ teaspoon salt
½ teaspoon horseradish
¼ teaspoon white pepper
1 tablespoon fresh lemon juice
¼ cup parsley
2 tablespoons fresh dill
1 cup salad oil or olive oil

In a food processor or blender mix all the ingredients, except the oil. Add the oil slowly until the mixture has thickened. Chill well and serve with the Grilled Shrimp and Scallops on Skewers.

Baked Whole Fish in Banana Leaves

1 whole firm fleshed fresh fish for baking or fresh salmon
Banana or ti leaves to cover the fish
Salt and pepper to taste
1 cup coconut cream
1 cup chopped Maui onions
½ cup chopped Chinese parsley
Cucumber, thinly sliced for garnish
Tomato, thinly sliced for garnish

Clean fish and pat dry with paper towels. Measure the thickness of the fish behind the gills and allow 10 minutes cooking time to the inch. Place the leaves on a cookie sheet, center the fish in the middle of the leaves and salt and pepper the fish. Combine coconut cream, Maui onions and parsley. Pour over the fish. Finish wrapping the leaves around the fish and place in an oven preheated to 350°F. Bake for determined cooking time. Remove the fish from the oven and carefully place on a heated platter. Garnish with thin slices of cucumber and tomatoes.

Island-Style Chili and Rice

1½ pounds coarse ground chuck roast
1½ pounds coarse ground pork butt
2 cups chopped onions
6 cloves garlic, minced
¼ cup chili seasoning
2 tablespoons oregano
¼ cup ground comino
2 tablespoons paprika
2 Hawaiian red chili peppers, seeded and chopped
½ cup chopped Chinese parsley
4 cups water or rich beef stock
Salt to taste
3 cups cooked pinto or kidney beans (optional)
Hot rice

In a large heavy pot place the beef, pork, onions, garlic, chili seasoning, oregano, comino, paprika, chili peppers and Chinese parsley. Pour water over the mixture and bring to a boil. Reduce heat and simmer for 1½ to 2 hours. Add additional water or broth, if needed. When the chili is cooked, skim off the fat. The chili can be made ahead to this point, then chilled. When ready to serve, heat the chili and add the beans if you are using them. Serve over hot rice.

Homemade Sausage for Grilling

1½ pounds lean pork, cut into 1-inch cubes and chilled
1 pound pork fat, cut into 1-inch cubes and chilled
½ pound lean beef, cut into 1-inch cubes and chilled
1 tablespoon Hawaiian salt
1½ teaspoons black pepper
1 tablespoon oregano
2 tablespoons basil
½ cup chopped parsley
1 tablespoon thyme
1 tablespoon fennel seed
2 tablespoons chopped garlic
½ to 1½ cups ice water (add more if the mixture will take it)
2 yards of hog casings, washed and drained. (the sausage may be rolled in cheesecloth if hog casings are not available)

Process the chilled meat in a food processor or grind very fine with a meat grinder. Place the ground meat in a large bowl. Mix the spices and herbs and blend well with the meat. Add ½ cup of ice water as you are mixing the meat. Keep adding ice water until the mixture will hold no more liquid. Chill the mixture for 24 hours. Fill the casing with chilled meat, or roll small amounts into links rolled in cheesecloth. Tie the sausage into long links. Grill over hot coals.

Crisp Duck with Mango and Cassis Sauce

2 fresh ducks (4 to 5 pounds each)
Salt and freshly ground black pepper
2 onions, cut in halves
2 oranges, cut in halves
4 firm ripe mangoes
¼ cup water
1 cup Cassis

Pat the ducks dry with paper towels; salt and pepper the cavities. Place the onions and oranges in the ducks and truss the ducks with cotton string. Prick the duck skin with a 2-tine carving or roasting fork. Place the ducks breast side up in a large roasting pan with a rack. Place in an oven preheated to 450°F and bake for 30 minutes. Turn the oven down to 400°F. Turn the ducks onto their breasts and bake for another 30 minutes. The last 30 minutes turn the ducks breast side up. Remove from the oven and allow to rest for 20 minutes While the ducks are resting make the mango sauce. Peel and slice the mangoes and place in a heavy saucepan with the water; simmer until they are tender but still hold their shape. Add the Cassis and simmer for about 5 minutes. Carve the ducks and arrange on a platter. Serve the mango sauce with the duck.

Duck Breasts with Guava Port Sauce

6 whole duck breasts, boned with the skin left on
Salt and freshly ground pepper to taste
Guava Port Sauce (recipe follows)

Cut the duck breasts in half and place skin side up on a roasting rack. Place the breasts in a preheated 450°F oven for 15 minutes. Remove the duck from the oven and reduce the heat to 300°F. Baste the duck breasts with Guava Port Sauce and return to the oven, basting every few minutes for the next 10 minutes. Remove the duck breasts from the rack to a cutting board and slice the breasts diagonally into fan shapes and arrange on warmed plates with a few tablespoons of sauce under the breasts to make a colorful presentation.

Guava Port Sauce

1 cup guava jelly
1 cup port wine

Combine the guava jelly and port wine in a small saucepan and simmer over low heat until the sauce is reduced by half.

Lilikoi Glazed Cornish Game Hens

4 Cornish hens, cleaned and trussed
Salt and pepper
1 jar (7 oz.) lilikoi jelly
2 tablespoons water

Preheat oven to 350°F. Rinse Cornish hens and pat dry with paper towels. Salt and pepper the hens and tie the legs and wings in close to the body with cotton string. Place the hens on a rack breast side down and bake for 30 minutes. At the end of 30 minutes turn the hens breast side up and baste with a little butter if the breasts seem dry. Bake the hens breast side up for another 30 minutes. Melt the lilikoi jelly and the water together. During the last 15 minutes of the baking time, increase the oven temperature to 425°F and baste the hens every 5 minutes with the lilikoi jelly mixture. Extra sauce may be passed when the hens are served.

Korean Barbecued Short Ribs

3 pounds beef short ribs
¾ cup soy sauce
2 tablespoons water
4 teaspoons sherry
1 teaspoon sesame oil
3 tablespoons brown sugar
2 cloves garlic, minced
½ teaspoon minced fresh ginger
2 tablespoons thinly sliced green onions
1 tablespoon toasted sesame seeds

Cut beef in ½-inch slices down to within ½ inch from bone. Combine remaining ingredients and pour over short ribs. Allow to marinate at least 1 hour before broiling. Broil 5 inches from broiler unit for 20 minutes; turning once. Makes 6 servings.

Chicken Long Rice Oriental

3 pounds chicken breasts
3 tablespoons oil
2 cloves garlic, minced
6 cups chicken broth
1 teaspoon minced fresh ginger or ¼ teaspoon powdered ginger
1½ tablespoons salt
2 bundles (1¾ oz. each) long rice
1 can (6 oz.) whole mushrooms, drained
2 tablespoons thinly sliced green onions

Remove skin and bones from chicken and use them to prepare the chicken broth. Cube chicken. Heat oil in a large skillet; saute chicken and garlic until just browned. Add broth, ginger and salt; simmer 1 hour or until chicken is tender. Soak long rice in warm water for 30 minutes; cut into 2 inch lengths. Add long rice and mushrooms to chicken; simmer 15 more minutes. Sprinkle with green onions just before serving. Makes 12 servings.

Idea: Chinese black mushrooms can be substituted for the canned whole mushrooms. If dried they should be soaked in warm water for 15 minutes, then discard stem and slice cap.

Chinese Baked Cabbage

1 head Chinese cabbage
1 pound ground pork
½ cup sliced green onions
1 tablespoon ginger juice*
¼ cup soy sauce
1 tablespoon cornstarch

Remove the root end of the Chinese cabbage and blanch the leaves in hot water until limp. Arrange the larger leaves in the bottom and around the sides of an ovenproof casserole. Preheat oven to 350°F. Combine ground pork, green onions, ginger juice, soy sauce and cornstarch; mix well. Place half the pork mixture in the center of the cabbage leaves. Cover with more cabbage leaves, add remaining filling and again cover with cabbage leaves. Cover the top of the casserole tightly with foil and bake for 30 to 40 minutes. When casserole is baked, remove from the oven and drain off any liquid that has collected. To this liquid add:

2 tablespoons soy sauce
2 tablespoons vinegar
2 tablespoons sugar
2 tablespoons cornstarch

Combine the soy sauce, vinegar, sugar and cornstarch together and stir into the liquid from the casserole. In a heavy pan cook the liquid over medium heat until thickened. Cover the casserole with a large plate and turn the contents out. Pour the thickened juices over the top and garnish with a few sprigs of Chinese parsley.

*Grate fresh ginger and squeeze out the juice in a piece of cheese cloth to make ginger juice.

Beef Broccoli Oriental

1 pound beef flank, partially frozen
1 teaspoon baking soda
¼ cup water
¼ cup soy sauce
2 tablespoons oyster sauce
1 teaspoon sesame oil
1 teaspoon sugar
1 teaspoon cornstarch
½ teaspoon salt
2 tablespoons oil
2 cups broccoli florets, blanched for 1 minute
3 green onions, cut into 2-inch lengths

Slice beef flank thinly across the grain. Add baking soda and water; let stand for several hours or overnight. Combine soy sauce, oyster sauce, sesame oil, sugar, cornstarch and salt; mix well and set aside. Heat a heavy pan or wok. Add oil and stir fry the meat until the pink color leaves; remove from wok. Add broccoli and green onions to the wok; toss for a few minutes, then return the meat to the wok. Add sauce to the meat and stir until the sauce thickens. Serve at once.

Idea: Serve with Toasted Noodle Cakes or hot steamed rice.

Grandma's Tofu and Pork Hash

2 blocks (8 oz. each) soft tofu
¼ pound ground pork
¼ cup green onion tops, cut into 2-inch lengths
1 tablespoon grated fresh ginger
1 tablespoon hot black bean paste
1 tablespoon sherry
½ teaspoon salt
2 tablespoons soy sauce
2 teaspoons cornstarch
1 tablespoon water
1 green onion, finely shredded

Cut tofu into small ½-inch cubes; set aside. In a heavy pan or wok stir fry pork. Add green onion tops. Combine ginger, hot black bean paste, sherry, salt, soy sauce, cornstarch and water; stir well. Add tofu to the pork and toss very carefully. Add the sauce and bring to a simmer. Remove to a deep dish and sprinkle with shredded green onion. Serve at once.

Fried Ginger Pork

2 pounds lean pork
¼ cup oil
1 cup finely minced Maui onions
2 cloves garlic, minced
½ cup soy sauce
1 tablespoon chopped fresh ginger
2 tablespoons vinegar
1 tablespoon black sesame seeds

Cut the pork into 1-inch cubes. Heat oil in a heavy skillet and saute pork on all sides, until it is nice and brown. Add onions and garlic and cook for 5 minutes. Stir in soy sauce, ginger and vinegar; cover the pan and simmer for 10 minutes. Sprinkle sesame seeds over the pork and serve with rice as a main dish or with foodpicks as a pupu.

Sauteed Pork Tenderloin with Mushroom and Cheese Topping

1 pound pork tenderloin, butterflied into 4 servings
½ cup flour
2 eggs
1 cup fresh bread crumbs
¼ cup clarified butter
1 cup sliced mushrooms
½ cup grated Swiss cheese
Salt and freshly ground black pepper
Mustard Cream Sauce (recipe follows)

Coat pork tenderloin with flour, then dip into beaten eggs. Coat with bread crumbs. Heat clarified butter in a heavy pan. Add the tenderloin and brown on both sides. The pork, when cooked, should be tender when the point of a sharp knife is inserted into the meat. Place pork on a platter and keep warm in a 200°F oven. Saute mushrooms in a little butter. When the mushrooms are just soft remove them from the pan and set aside. Top each serving of pork with mushrooms and 2 tablespoons of the grated cheese. Turn the oven up to 350°F. Heat the pork until the cheese melts. Serve with Mustard Cream Sauce.

Mustard Cream Sauce

½ cup chopped shallots
¼ cup butter
2 cups rich beef stock
1 teaspoon tomato paste
1 tablespoon Dijon style mustard
½ cup heavy cream
2 tablespoons Madeira

Saute shallots in butter. Add stock and reduce the liquid by half. Add tomato paste, mustard and cream. Bring liquid to a simmer and add Madeira. Adjust seasonings to taste. Serve with Sauteed Pork Tenderloin with Mushroom and Cheese Topping.

Pork Loin Roast with Mangoes

5 to 6 pound pork loin roast
Salt and pepper
⅓ cup raspberry or Balsamic vinegar
3 cups sliced firm ripe mangoes

Preheat the oven to 350°F. Place the pork in a shallow baking pan on a rack. Salt and pepper the meat and place in the center of the rack with the fat side on top. Pour vinegar over the mangoes; set aside. Roast for 1½ hours. Remove the pork from the baking pan and place on an ovenproof dish. Pour the mangoes and vinegar over the meat and return it to the oven. Roast for 30 minutes more or until meat thermometer registers 165°F. Remove meat from the oven and allow to rest for 20 minutes. Slice the roast and present on a warmed platter. Spoon the extra sauce over the pork. Garnish with watercress or parsley. Serve warm.

VEGETABLE DISHES

Lush Hawaiian Waterfalls, ISLAND OF HAWAII

Stir Fry Eggplant

4 to 5 long eggplants
1 teaspoon salt
2 tablespoons oil
2 cloves garlic, minced
1 teaspoon hot chili pepper flakes
½ cup mint leaves
½ cup chicken broth
1 teaspoon cornstarch

Cut eggplant into ½-inch diagonal slices; sprinkle with salt and let stand for 20 minutes. Heat a heavy pan or wok; add the oil. Pat eggplant dry with paper towels. Add eggplant to the hot oil, toss lightly. Add garlic and pepper flakes; stir fry. Add mint leaves. Dissolve cornstarch in chicken broth; add to eggplant and stir well. Cook until the sauce thickens. Serve at once.

Ginger Stir Fried Zucchini

3 medium zucchini
2 tablespoons oil
1 teaspoon sugar
2 tablespoons soy sauce
1 tablespoon grated fresh ginger
½ teaspoon salt
1 teaspoon sesame oil

Cut zucchini into ¼-inch thick julienne strips. Heat oil in a heavy pan or wok. Add zucchini and toss gently for 1 minute. Add all the remaining ingredients and stir fry for another few seconds or until the sauce is hot.

Idea: Carrots and/or leeks may be substituted for the zucchini.

Baked Zucchini Casserole

4 to 5 small zucchini, sliced ½-inch thick
2 small onions, sliced
4 firm ripe tomatoes, cut into wedges
½ cup chopped parsley
¼ cup fresh basil leaves
Salt and pepper to taste
2 cups grated Swiss cheese

Preheat oven to 350°F. Place vegetables and herbs in an ovenproof casserole. Sprinkle with salt and pepper. Cover and bake for 45 minutes or microwave on high power for 12 minutes. Remove the cover the last 15 minutes of baking and add the cheese. Return to the oven. Serve with hot French bread as a vegetarian meal or as a side dish.

Idea: 1 tablespoon chopped garlic may be added to the recipe, if desired.

Kahuku Corn Fritters

½ cup water
2 tablespoons butter
½ cup flour
2 large eggs
2 tablespoons chopped green onions
Salt and pepper to taste
1½ cups fresh corn kernels
¼ cup clarified butter

In a heavy saucepan bring water and butter to a boil. Add flour all at one time and stir continually until the dough pulls away from the sides of the pan. Add eggs one at a time, beating well after each addition. Stir in green onions, salt, pepper and corn. Chill until ready to use. Heat clarified butter in a heavy pan. Drop the fritter batter ¼ cup at a time into the pan. Brown well on each side, about 3 to 4 minutes per side. Serve with sausages, maple syrup, apple sauce, melted guava jelly or sour cream. Makes 4 servings.

Maui Onions in Onion Sauce

12 small Maui onions or small yellow onions
6 tablespoons butter
¼ cup flour
2 cups milk
1 cup chopped green onions
1 teaspoon salt
½ teaspoon white pepper
2 cups grated Swiss cheese

Preheat oven to 350°F. Peel onions and make a cross cut on the stem of each. Butter an ovenproof casserole with 2 tablespoons of the butter. Place onions in one layer in the casserole. Cover with a lid or foil and bake for 45 minutes. In a heavy saucepan melt the remaining 4 tablespoons of butter. Add flour and cook until the mixture is light and bubbly. Stir in milk and cook until the sauce has thickened. Add green onions, salt and pepper to the sauce. Remove the onions from the oven. Pour the sauce over the onions, sprinkle the top with grated cheese and return, uncovered, to the oven. Bake 15 minutes longer. Serve hot.

Kauai Taro Pancakes

4 cups grated fresh taro (about 1½ pounds)
2 eggs, beaten
⅓ cup flour
¼ cup grated Maui onion
Salt and pepper
¼ cup clarified butter

Grate taro and boil in salted water for 5 minutes; drain well. Combine taro, eggs, flour, onion, salt and pepper; mix well. Heat clarified butter in a heavy pan. Drop the batter ½ cup at a time into the pan; shape into flat pancakes. Brown well on each side. Serve with butter or any of your favorite toppings. Great accompanied with spicy sausage. Makes 4 servings.

Kona Tomato Casserole

8 large firm ripe tomatoes
½ cup chopped Chinese parsley
2 tablespoons finely chopped garlic
Salt and freshly ground pepper
¼ cup olive oil

Preheat oven to 325°F. Cut tomatoes in half and arrange in an ovenproof dish. Sprinkle with Chinese parsley and garlic. Season lightly with salt and pepper. Sprinkle olive oil over the top and bake for 1 hour. Tomatoes may be cooked longer if you wish them to be drier. Serve with broiled or grilled meats.

RICE AND NOODLES

Kohala Coast, ISLAND OF HAWAII

Rice Pilaf with Toasted Macadamia Nuts

¼ cup olive oil
2 cups long grain rice
3 cups rich chicken stock
½ cup chopped onion
2 cloves garlic, finely chopped
1 cup golden raisins
1 tablespoon paprika
1 teaspoon grated lemon zest
1 tablespoon salt
½ teaspoon freshly ground black pepper
1 tablespoon olive oil
½ cup chopped macadamia nuts
1 tablespoon chopped parsley

In a flame-proof casserole heat the ¼ cup olive oil; add the rice and stir until golden brown. Bring chicken stock to a boil; pour into casserole. Add onion and garlic; stir in raisins, paprika, lemon zest, salt and pepper. Cover the casserole and cook over low heat, about 25 minutes, or until the rice is done. While rice is cooking put the 1 tablespoon olive oil in a heavy pan and cook the macadamia nuts until golden brown. When the rice is cooked toss the nuts with the rice and serve at once. Sprinkle with chopped parsley.

Mango Rice

¼ cup clarified butter
3 tablespoons chopped onion
1 bay leaf
1½ cups long grain rice
1 cup boiling chicken stock
Salt to taste
2 firm ripe mangoes, diced

Preheat oven to 325°F. In a flame-proof casserole melt the clarified butter. Add the onion and bay leaf, stir for a few minutes, then add the rice. Stir the rice until well coated with butter. Allow the rice to just become golden. Add the boiling stock and salt. Cover the casserole and bake for 18 to 20 minutes. Remove from the oven and stir in the mangoes.

Pasta with Sesame Seed Sauce

½ cup sesame seeds
1 cup rich chicken stock
3 tablespoons dry sherry
3 tablespoons soy sauce
2 tablespoons honey
1 tablespoon sesame oil
1 tablespoon hoisin sauce
1 tablespoon tomato paste
Thin pasta

In a heavy saucepan lightly brown the sesame seeds. Reserve 2 tablespoons whole sesame seeds and grind remaining seeds into a powder. In the saucepan combine sesame seed powder, chicken stock, dry sherry, soy sauce, honey, sesame oil, hoisin sauce and tomato paste; simmer until slightly thickened and smooth. Cook pasta as directed on package; drain and toss with the sesame sauce. Sprinkle with reserved sesame seeds. Garnish with shredded green onions, if desired. May be served hot or cold.

Toasted Noodle Cakes

1 quart water
1 pkg. (10 oz.) saimin noodles
½ teaspoon salt
5 tablespoons salad oil

Bring water to a boil; add noodles and salt. Reduce heat to simmer and cook noodles about 2 minutes or until barely tender. Rinse under cold water; drain. Mix noodles with 2 tablespoons of the oil. Heat remaining 3 tablespoons of the oil in a large skillet. Add noodles; spread to cover bottom of pan. On medium heat, brown noodles on underside; turn and brown other side. Remove from skillet and cut into 6 servings.

Gon Lo Mein

2 tablespoons oil
1 onion, thinly sliced
2 stalks celery, sliced diagonally
½ pound char siu, cut into 2-inch strips
1 pound chow mein noodles
¼ pound bean sprouts
3 green onions, thinly sliced
1 tablespoon sesame oil
2 tablespoons soy sauce
3 tablespoons oyster sauce
1 tablespoon sugar

Heat wok to high heat and add oil. Stir fry onion, celery and char siu for 2 to 3 minutes. Add noodles, bean sprouts, green onions and sesame oil; cook for 3 minutes. Combine soy sauce, oyster sauce and sugar; add to noodles. Toss lightly to mix. Sprinkle with sesame seeds. Makes 4 to 6 servings.

CONDIMENTS

Iao Needle, MAUI

Mango Chutney

8 to 10 large green mangoes
2 teaspoons salt
1 cup golden raisins
1 cup dark rum
4 cups dark brown sugar
4 cups vinegar (cider or malt)
Zest of 3 limes, cut in thin strips
½ cup grated fresh ginger
1 teaspoon red pepper flakes
2 teaspoons allspice
1 teaspoon ground comino
4 cloves garlic, minced

Peel and cut the mangoes into thin strips or slices. Sprinkle with the salt and set aside. Soak the raisins in rum. Place the mangoes in a heavy saucepan; add brown sugar, vinegar and lime zest. Cook over medium heat for 10 minutes. Add all the spices and cook slowly for 30 minutes. Add the raisins and the rum and cook for 5 minutes. Pour into sterilized jars. Cool and refrigerate.

Fresh Cucumber, Tomato and Onion Chutney

1 cucumber, peeled, seeded and chopped
3 ripe tomatoes, peeled, seeded and chopped
1 Maui onion, cut in half and thinly sliced
2 cloves garlic, finely chopped
¼ cup chopped Chinese parsley
¼ cup fresh lime juice
1 seeded and chopped Hawaiian red chili pepper
Salt and pepper to taste

Combine all the ingredients; mix well. Chill. Serve with seafood, hamburgers and tacos.

Pineapple Chutney

1 quart fresh or canned pineapple
4 cups chopped onion
2 cups golden raisins
2½ cups white vinegar
3 cups brown sugar
1 tablespoon salt
½ cup grated fresh ginger
1 tablespoon mustard seed
2 tablespoons seeded and chopped Hawaiian chili peppers
1 tablespoon tumeric
Zest of 1 orange, cut in thin strips
Zest of 1 lemon, cut in thin strips

Combine all the ingredients in a heavy saucepan and simmer for 1 hour. Pour into sterilized jars. Cool and refrigerate. The chutney is best if it ages for about 1 month in the refrigerator.

Ambrosia Conserve

2 navel oranges
1 large pineapple
6 tart green apples
Lemon juice to taste
2 cups water
1 cup golden raisins
6 cups sugar
1 cup grated coconut

Cut zest from oranges, remove the white inner membrane. Cut zest into very thin strips. Section the oranges. Peel pineapple; remove core and cut into cubes. Core apples; slice. In a heavy saucepan combine pineapple, apples, lemon juice and water; bring to a boil and cook for 10 minutes. Add orange zest, golden raisins and sugar. Return to a boil and cook until the sugar dissolves. Add coconut and oranges. Simmer for 30 minutes, stirring frequently. Pour into four 1 pint sterilized jars. Seal and invert jars until cool. Serve with duck, game and pork roasts.

DESSERTS AND BREADS

Skiing—Mauna Kea, ISLAND OF HAWAII

Vanilla Ice Cream

4 eggs, separated
1½ cups sugar
½ teaspoon salt
2 cups milk
2 cups half and half
1 tablespoon vanilla
4 cups whipping cream

Beat the egg yolks; add sugar and salt and place in a double boiler. Whisk in 1 cup of the milk and stir until the sugar is dissolved. Add the remaining milk, half and half, vanilla and heavy cream; chill for several hours or overnight. When ready to make the ice cream, pour the chilled mixture into the canister. Assemble the ice cream maker and place in the ice pail. Start with 4 cups of crushed ice and 1 cup coarse ice cream salt. Continue with this 4-to-1 ratio until the pail is full. Start to crank the ice cream in a slow but steady motion. After churning the mixture for 10 to 15 minutes, whip the egg whites until they hold firm peaks. Carefully open the canister and add the egg whites to the now partially frozen mixture. Continue cranking until the ice cream feels very firm. Remove the top from the canister, be very careful not to get any salt mixture inside, clean off the paddles and return the lid. Put a cork or other stopper in the hole. Fill the pail with ice and salt and allow to stand for an hour. If this is not convenient, place the ice cream in containers and freeze until ready to use. Or . . . just scoop the ice cream into bowls when you are through churning and serve. Makes 2 quarts.

Macadamia Nut Ice Cream

Add 1 cup Kahlua liqueur and 1½ cups chopped macadamia nuts when you add the beaten egg whites in the Vanilla Ice Cream recipe.

Chocolate Ice Cream

Using the Vanilla Ice Cream recipe, add 10 ounces chopped semi-sweet chocolate to the egg yolk and milk mixture in the double boiler. Stir until the chocolate has melted.

Strawberry Ice Cream

Blend 1 pint ripe fresh sliced strawberries with ½ cup of the sugar from the above recipe. Add ½ cup Grand Marnier, if desired. Add the strawberries when you add the beaten egg whites in the Vanilla Ice Cream recipe.

Macadamia Nut Cookies

1¼ cups butter
1¼ cups powdered sugar
1 egg
2 teaspoons vanilla
1⅓ cups flour
¼ teaspoon salt
1½ cups chopped macadamia nuts

Preheat oven to 350°F. Lightly grease baking sheets. Cream butter and powdered sugar. Add egg and vanilla; beat until light. Sift together flour and salt; gradually add to creamed mixture. Stir in macadamia nuts. Drop teaspoonfuls of batter onto prepared baking sheets and bake for 15 to 20 minutes. Makes 48.

Guava Strawberry Bars

¾ cup butter
¾ cup brown sugar
1½ cups flour
1 teaspoon baking powder
½ teaspoon salt
2 cups rolled oats
1 cup guava jam
1 cup strawberry jam

Preheat oven to 350°F. Combine butter and brown sugar until light and fluffy. Add flour, baking powder, salt and rolled oats; mix well. Press half of the mixture into a 9 x 9-inch pan. Mix together guava and strawberry jam. Spread the guava strawberry jam over the dough and cover with the remaining dough. Bake for 30 minutes or until golden brown. Cool slightly before cutting into squares.

Lemon Coconut Bars

2 cups flour
½ cup powdered sugar
½ pound unsalted sweet cream butter

Preheat oven to 350°F. In a food processor or with your fingers blend the flour, powdered sugar and butter until it clings together. Press into a 9 x 13-inch pan. Bake until lightly brown, about 20 to 25 minutes.

Filling

4 eggs
1 cup sugar
½ cup lemon juice
1 tablespoon lemon zest
2 cups grated coconut
¼ cup flour
1 teaspoon baking powder

Beat together eggs and sugar until light and fluffy. Stir in the remaining ingredients and pour over the baked crust. Bake for 20 to 25 minutes longer. Allow to cool slightly, then spread with glaze.

Glaze

1 cup powdered sugar
2 tablespoons melted butter
2 tablespoons lemon juice

Combine powdered sugar, melted butter and lemon juice; mix well. Spread on filling.

Banana Muffins with Guava Butter

2 cups flour
1 tablespoon baking powder
¼ cup sugar
½ teaspoon salt
2 teaspoons cinnamon
1 cup milk
⅓ cup butter, melted
1 egg, beaten
¾ cup mashed ripe banana
2 teaspoons grated orange zest
Guava Butter (recipe follows)

Preheat oven to 400°F. Sift together flour, baking powder, sugar, salt and cinnamon. Make a well in the center of the flour mixture and add milk, butter, egg, banana and orange zest. Mix just enough to moisten the dry ingredients. Batter will be lumpy. Oil a 12 portion muffin tin or use paper liners. Fill each section a little over half full. Bake for 20 to 25 minutes or until golden brown. Serve with Guava Butter while the muffins are hot.

Guava Butter

½ pound unsalted sweet cream butter, softened
½ cup guava jam

Combine butter and guava jam; mix until well blended. Chill until ready to use.

Baked Apples with Pineapple Filling

6 large apples
½ cup crushed pineapple, drained
¼ cup golden raisins
¾ cup guava jelly, melted

Core apples and score around the center. Place apples in a shallow ovenproof dish. Add about ½ inch of water or white wine. Stir together pineapple and raisins; divide the filling between the apples. Pour 2 tablespoons of the melted jelly over each apple. Place in an oven preheated to 350°F and bake until the apples are tender, about 30 to 60 minutes. Baste from time to time as the apples are cooking. When baked place the apples in small dishes and spoon over any liquid that is in the pan; chill.

Idea:

Use canned or homemade cranberry sauce. To each cup of sauce add 1 tablespoon of orange zest and 2 tablespoons of dark rum. Bake as above.

or

Combine ½ cup mincemeat with ½ cup chopped macadamia nuts and bake as above. Serve with whipped cream and a sprinkle of nutmeg on top.

Pineapple Bread Pudding

1 quart milk
4 cups Portuguese sweet bread cubes
2 tablespoons butter at room temperature
6 eggs
1½ cups sugar
2 tablespoons vanilla
1 cup golden raisins
1 cup crushed pineapple, drained

Preheat oven to 325°F. In a large bowl pour milk over the sweet bread cubes and let stand for 1 hour. Butter a 13 x 9 x 2-inch pan; set aside. Beat together eggs, sugar and vanilla and pour over the bread mixture. Stir in raisins and pineapple. Pour mixture into the prepared pan. Bake about 1 hour or until a knife inserted in the center of the pudding comes out clean. You may wish to sprinkle the top of the baked pudding with ½ cup powdered sugar when you remove it from the oven.

Paradise Chiffon Pie

3 ripe bananas
⅓ cup fresh lime juice
1 teaspoon finely grated lime zest
1 cup sugar
4 eggs, separated
2 envelopes plain gelatin
¼ cup cold water
1 cup whipping cream
1 9-inch baked pie shell
½ cup toasted chopped macadamia nuts

Mash bananas. Combine bananas, lime juice, lime zest, ½ cup of the sugar and egg yolks; mix well and place in the top of a double boiler. Cook over simmering water until the mixture thickens. Soften gelatin in cold water. Add softened gelatin to banana mixture and stir until dissolved. Remove from heat and chill until partly set. Beat egg whites until stiff. Gradually add the remaining ½ cup of the sugar. Beat cream to firm peak stage; fold into the banana mixture, then fold in the egg whites. Spoon into baked pie shell. Sprinkle with macadamia nuts; chill well. Makes 6 servings.

Coconut Cream Meringue Pie

2 cups milk
6 eggs, separated
1¼ cups sugar
½ cup flour
1½ cups toasted grated coconut
½ envelope plain gelatin
2 tablespoons cold water
1 cup whipping cream
1 teaspoon vanilla
1 9-inch baked pie shell

Scald milk until tiny bubbles form around the edge. Beat egg yolks with ½ cup of the sugar until light. Add flour and beat until smooth. This may be done in the food processor. Slowly pour the hot milk into the egg mixture; pour through a strainer back into the saucepan. Stirring with a wire whisk, bring mixture to a full boil and continue stirring until the mixture is very thick. Remove from heat and stir in 1¼ cups of the toasted coconut. Set aside to cool. Place gelatin in the cold water to soften. Heat the gelatin mixture over hot water until the gelatin is melted. Whip cream until firm peaks are formed. Add gelatin mixture and vanilla. Fold cream into the cool pastry cream. Spoon into the baked pie shell. Cover with meringue. Make meringue by beating egg whites, that are at room temperature, until firm peaks are formed. Add the remaining ¾ cup of the sugar, 1 tablespoon at a time, until the sugar has been used. Cover the pie filling to the edges of the crust with the meringue and mound up in the middle. Sprinkle the remaining ¼ cup of the toasted coconut over the meringue. Place in an oven preheated to 425°F. Bake 4 to 5 minutes or until the meringue is golden brown. Remove from the oven and cool on a rack.

Note: Toasted chopped macadamia nuts may be substituted for the toasted coconut.

Passion Fruit Sponge Cake

4 eggs, separated
¾ cup sugar
¾ cup cornstarch
¼ cup flour
1 teaspoon baking powder
2 cups passion fruit juice
1½ cups whipping cream
2 cups powdered sugar, sifted
1 teaspoon lemon juice

Preheat oven to 350°F. Butter and flour two 8-inch round cake pans. Tap the pans to remove any excess flour; set aside. Beat egg whites until firm peaks are formed; add sugar gradually and continue beating. Add the egg yolks, one at a time, and continue beating. Sift together cornstarch, flour and baking powder. Fold into the egg mixture with a large spatula or ballon whisk. Divide the mixture evenly between the two pans. Bake for 20 to 25 minutes. Do not overbake. Remove from the oven and cool 2 to 3 minutes before turning the cakes out on wire racks to cool. In a small saucepan simmer passion fruit juice until reduced to 1 cup. If you are using fresh passion fruit there is no need to reduce it. Whip cream until it holds firm peaks, then gradually add ⅓ cup of the reduced juice. Layer the filling between the cooled cake layers. Combine powdered sugar and lemon juice. Stir in enough of the reduced passion fruit juice to make a frosting of spreadable consistency. Pour the mixture over the top of the cake and quickly spread to a smooth finish. Refrigerate until ready to serve.

Coconut Fruit Cake

1 cup candied pineapple
1 cup candied orange peel
½ cup candied cherries
½ cup fresh lemon juice
1 cup sugar
½ cup butter
4 eggs, separated
1 cup toasted slivered almonds
1½ cups shredded coconut
¼ cup dark rum
¼ cup brandy
1¾ cups flour
2 teaspoons baking powder
1 cup golden raisins

Rinse candied fruit and pat dry with paper towels. Pour lemon juice over the fruit and allow to stand overnight. Cream together sugar and butter until light and fluffy. Add egg yolks and blend well. Stir in the almonds, coconut, rum and brandy. Sift together flour and baking powder; fold into the fruit mixture. Beat egg whites until they hold firm peaks, then fold into the flour mixture with a large spatula. Cut the fruit into small pieces, sprinkle with a little flour, and fold into the flour mixture along with the raisins. Pour into a buttered and paper lined 9-inch spring form pan. Place in the center of an oven preheated to 325°F and bake for 2½ hours. Allow to cool for several hours before serving.

Portuguese Sweet Bread

½ cup warm water (105°F or 115°F)
3 envelopes active dry yeast
1¾ cups sugar
1 cup mashed potatoes
½ cup warm milk
1 tablespoon salt
8 eggs
½ cup melted butter
¼ teaspoon grated nutmeg
7 cups flour

Combine warm water, yeast and ¼ cup of the sugar; set aside to proof. Combine mashed potatoes, warm milk and salt; add to the yeast mixture. Beat eggs with the remaining 1½ cups of the sugar until light. Add melted butter and nutmeg. Place flour in a large mixing bowl and make a well in the center. Pour in the potato and egg mixtures. Gradually work the liquid and flour together until a sticky mass is formed. Sprinkle flour on a work area, turn the dough from the bowl on to the floured area and knead until smooth and elastic. Return the dough to the bowl and allow to double in volume. Butter four 9 x 5 x 3-inch loaf pans. When the dough has doubled in volume, divide into four equal parts. Shape into loaves and place in the buttered pans. Allow the loaves to double in volume again. Preheat oven to 350°F. Prepare egg wash by beating together 1 egg and 1 tablespoon cold water. When loaves are ready to be baked, brush the top of each loaf with egg wash and sprinkle with a little sugar. Place in the oven and bake for 45 to 60 minutes. When done, the bread should sound hollow when tapped on the bottom. Remove the baked bread from the oven and cool on racks.

Pineapple Muffins

1½ cups flour
1 tablespoon baking powder
½ cup sugar
½ cup butter, melted
2 eggs
⅓ cup honey
1½ cups bran cereal
1 teaspoon salt
1 cup cream
1 cup crushed pineapple, well drained

Preheat oven to 375°F. Sift together flour, baking powder and sugar. Cream together butter, eggs and honey; stir in flour mixture, bran cereal, salt, cream and crushed pineapple until just mixed. Oil muffin pans and fill each section a little over half full. Bake for 20 to 25 minutes or until golden brown. Makes 20 muffins.

Baked Papaya with Fruit and Meringue

1 firm ripe papaya
½ cup whole green seedless grapes
1 kiwi fruit, peeled and sliced
1 cup pineapple chunks
1 cup fresh strawberries, sliced
6 tablespoons Grand Marnier
3 egg whites at room temperature
6 tablespoons sugar

Cut papaya into half lengthwise; remove seeds. Combine grapes, kiwi fruit, pineapple chunks, strawberries and 5 tablespoons of the Grand Marnier; toss lightly to mix. Fill papaya halves with the fruit; chill. When ready to serve, preheat oven to 450°F. Beat egg whites until firm peaks are formed. Add the sugar, 1 tablespoon at a time, until the sugar has been used. Fold in the remaining 1 tablespoon of the Grand Marnier. Pile the mergingue on the papayas and brown in the oven for 2 to 3 minutes. Serve at once. Makes 2 servings.

INDEX